CULTURAL SINGULARITY

ANDREW K. COYNE

CONTENTS:

BOOKI : Politics in Culture/Final Page

BOOKII: Snake-Charmers of the West

BOOKIII: Euphoria Morning

BOOKIV: (En)trance

BOOKV: Trans-mission

BOOKVI: Poetry
Idol of the Spiders Web
Rites of the Harvest
On Casuistry

BOOK I.

POLITICS IN CULTURE/ FINALPAGE

As they turn to the last page of the book, the reader realizes they have simultaneously, and not coincidentally, come to an end themselves. They have been completed, like the final chapter and the book itself, to a state of finality. Returning to the title page, "Politics in Culture", they are intoxicated with the temptation to read the book again, if only to sustain

their existence as a free
individual in a nation State on
the brink of assured
annihilation through implosion;
Inwardly regressing to an
Alpha-Point so far removed from
the meaning of the politick,
from the meaning of culture and
identity, from meaning itself.
The urge, however, like the
assuredness of the finality at
hand, ceases like a Spectre.
The text, the content, and
future of Politics, like the
reader, have no future, for in

the Cyber-Political-Cultural
Implosion all context is a
tomorrow with no beginning, and
a message failed to send to the
21st century that it's
theatrical debut has been
cancelled.

    What will instead replace
the individual, cultural,
political Mass? The
digitisation, the cross
terminal cybernetic ecstasy of
re-creation. The spectacle of
awe, the circus of humanity,

will ceaselessly attempt to
reverse engineer itself with
it's mythos-fable-romantick of
a past that never was.
Ironically, this failure, this
botched launch, will not be
televised, for this round of
production is a naked assertion
that it is not failing, but
failing again, in a closed
circuit that, like the computer
terminal in it's face, cannot
film itself, unless through the
mirror of the genii, the ghost
in the machine. It is this

ghost, this apparition, which
gives the illusion of a
History, the illusion of a Past
with true meaning. The illusion
of a real, unfolding
sequentially over time with an
Omega-Point of either progress
or destruction. Neither ever
were, for time was not, and
time will not be by our side,
but rather forever out of our
reach like the Apex in the
mythology of Sisyphus. We are
the outsiders of a world self-
created. The politick captures

this estrangement best, for it was the godhead of the last round of self delusion we all called reality. The hyperreal will only be yet another false God for the philosopher of the now. This too is a construct as fictional as a cherry tree and as harmful as an axe.

The hyperreal as substitute reality; The postmodern, de-contructionist, self-complimentary reassertion of Romanticism. Is not postmodernity a reflective statement of detachment from modernity? Is not this reflection of distance from, or birth away from the "other" with the "other" being all things past, not Romantic in nature and essence? Furthermore, was not Romanticism birthed from the Roman? With its pomp, excess, blood-letting, the Holy Roman was post-epochal at it's height. The Roman Law, the Nero's, the filthy water at its terminus, the orgy of Church and State, this was the statuary of culture left to remain to the annals of a History that would absorb and dissolve itself and imbibe its spectacle within the modern culture-warfare. The so called radicals of post-modernity were no more than historians; claiming opposition to the idea of a living history, they were no less the bearers of a critique on a history to come, one of the future. This future,

sadly for the postmodern
reader, is just another Round
in the Nihilistic Eternal
Return. For although it was
shouted from the rooftops that
God is dead, the eternal return
within the structure that
announced this outburst,
concludes that all things
return in a cyclic rhythm, such
as the manavantaras of the
Eastern Yogi. Upsetting to the
aesthetics of atheism with
nihilism in its quiver, the
dying or dead God must return

again and again, over and over,
cycle after cycle, in rhythmic
cessation. Is the utterance of
postmodernity then that "The
Dying God has Returned?"
Likewise, should it be evident,
at least as a corollary, that
if it is not necessary, it
appears sufficient to say that
"The Dying Modern has
Returned." Or further, "The
Roman has Returned." If so, if
all roads lead to Rome once
again, what will signal the
fall, or prevent it?

The West has prided itself as the New Rome from its Democratic Origins. Yet, what measures where taken in checks and balances in say, The Federalist Papers, beyond suppressing the fires of intrigue and cabal, at preventing the corruption of the Priesthood? For, although like any other historical epoch, debate is open to the causes and nature of events, it is widely known the corruption of the Priesthood signaled the Fall of Rome. The Mystery Schools that later transmuted and rose like a Phoenix to the high seat of governance, degraded and poisoned both pauper and Pontiff. Regardless, any safety measures against such an event or non-event from happening to the Priesthood itself is not the issue. The Priesthood simply stood as the cultural barometer of Reality given its Universality and Totality. The Priesthood is

our Media. This nebulous Medusa
with snake tongues reaching
every aspect of the cultus, the
modern or postmodern culture is
in a stasis of total
entanglement from the data
server of infinite modules, and
yet in the hands of so few this
resembles Priesthood. Should
the Federalist Papers not have
been so enwrapped in protecting
Free-Speech, but rather in
protecting the dissemination of
speech, that is Media? Like
the right to bear arms, the

20th/21st century, with its
semi-automatic weapons, begs
the question is it worth
inquiring the intentions of the
Founding Fathers of the West
from a world so far removed
from the musket? Yet, if our
analogy of Media as Priesthood
holds water, then this was well
within their minds given the
emphasis on Separation of
Church and State. Nonetheless,
although separated legally,
their strict connection
demonstrates how powerful both

Church and State were to be held. It is Structure against Culture that defines the two polarities of the Church/State issue. The question then is, what measures were taken to Preserve the Culture? Upsetting to the Mass of society, all measures were taken. The State, The Priesthood, our Media Medusa, all of these were birthed, like Romulus and Remus, from an unseen and impossibly small fraction/faction of the

populous.   This,   all long
preceding the industrio-
emergance of the middle-class
which would ultimately attempt
to peer into the looking-glass
of said faction. The haves and
the have-nots has always been a
childish derogation of the
global population. Still, the
playground definition holds
true, and as in Rome, the Birth
of the West solely sought to
preserve the hands that hold
Medusa, not the billions that

her tongues encircle like the
Ouroboros.

    Regardless of any ominous
or nefarious master plan to
subjugate the Mass of Society,
it still need be answered what
will become of this Mass, this
ethereal global network of
receivers and doers we call
Society as a cultural value?
Moreover, what value will be
left, what standard of
individuation or individuality
remains when the Culture is

compromised? It appears the
Culture has been hijacked from
within it's own network. This
inside job, the eradication of
a culture by a culture of
annihilation, is not novel. As
mentioned, the cyclic undoing
of a culture is rhythmic.
Hegemony is the prime mover of
this uninterrupted arc.
Culture annihilates vying
culture through means of war.
Often absorbing the dying
culture, the victor
emerges anew with its amended

Gods, amended morals, amended laws etc. This unravels war by war until the Hegemon Is Culture. Only yesterdays globalization offered a glimpse at what this resembled in a historic sense. For we are past globalization, post-globalization, and rather pre-singularity or singularity itself. This singularity, from a cultural sense, is defined by the totality of value. Value as removed from any economic, political, moral, linguistic, or legal exchange. It is value as exchange. The singularity of value as exchange is Universal and One-Dimensional. No nation or individual can escape the world of singularity, as one in a Romantic Past could head for the Mountain-top, because in this matrix of value as exchange, any such action would only be part of that exchange. That exchange of removal from culture, the "hermit", is still a piece of the exchange value of the singularity, given, ironically, it's romantic escape-act is only one of infinite story-lines now a fable-omnipresent in the Singularity. It is through this omnipresence, that all exchange by sign or symbol, by gesture or utterance, by art or custom, by law or disorder equals the totality of value. Thus, every exchange is value, and every value is exchange in totality.

Any Neo-Marxist, Post-Capitalist angle on the singular nature of the cultural web is dismissed as they too are simply swallowed like Jonah into the whale of the singularity. All ideas have led to this endless apex of culture. The ever-expanding circumference of Pascal seems fitting as the nature of the singularity will never change yet ever expand; its expansion including its terminal and origin points in the rhythm of

the Eternal Return. How can
one be so sure that culture as
we know it has reached an
Omega-Point of infinite
variation? By definition,
culture is a cultus or group
within a larger group. What we
have before us is the cultus
expanding to a point where it
is Universal, Total, Singular.
There is no plurality but an
entity of interstitial
connection points strewn upon
dimension points in space
traversing a pseudo-timeline

that scientists claim is
relative at best. Politics,
Economies, Races, Religions,
all have blended and unfolded
into a spectrum of thought only
held in existence by their use-
value to the Media-Cultus of
the Unknown Dawn. This silent
Revolution, this re-volving,
was the doing of the techno-
dynamism of the end of the 20th
Century and the finite nature
of the planet itself. The
Unknown Dawn no longer ravages
economies of style, but rather

bolts to new horizons in
space.

BOOK II.

SNAKE-CHARMERS OF THE WEST

Silicon Valley of the Gods,
or Silicon Death Valley? This
question of merit or crime is
omnipresent in the digital-
techno-spectacle of the present
cultural rhythm or decline.
Tech companies have given us
access to a wealth of
information yet at the price of
a click. Polling, advertising,
focus-groups, clinical tech-
trials, all of these media seek
to withdraw the mystery of the
psyche, the psychological
dynamic of the 20th Century to

a place of consumer value. Yet every exchange is value and every value is exchange in totality. Hence, these cross-demographic manufacturing modules only behave as an exchange of exchange-values implanted into the study modules themselves. It is X screening X. It is the mirror of capitalism; the place where monetization seeks monetization via monetizing individual psyche profiles at the cost of creating anew, a sector of new

psyche profiles only in need of
more screening modules and
tech-assessment for they have

been "viewed" and hence
altered according to quantum
mechanics. This endless

observation could be called the
Observation Of Infinity(by the
Snake-charmers of the West).
Observing Infinity, or the
viewing of the speed of
Cultural transfiguration
creates a sense of buoyancy and
weightlessness since it is
orbital at this stage of
Cultural Singularity. It is
orbital in many ways. By its
nature, culture now is
predetermined on a 24 hour
clock turned endlessly via a
vast and pervasive network of

satellites literally orbiting the planet. Also, by its action, or rather its behavioral movement. It is drawn in by the gravity of its implosion. To be clear, this is in opposition to a cultural explosion, where culture would permeate all ends of the earth in diverse and manifold constructs. It simply is the inward, or esoteric, in-drawing of the cultus to a primordial ocean of nothingness. Not to be confused with a Nirvana or

Samadhi of blank expression,
this is a highly complex
circuit-board of infinite
expressions that yet are void
of meaning on a cultural(as the
cultus of history is
understood) level and on a
cultural degree. There is no
spectrum for instance, to say
we are at the brink of a loss
of culture, of politics, of
religion, of education, of
economics, of gender, of art,
or of any pseudo-cultural
factor or signifier. The

spectrum is closed to the
ultimacy of culture as
singular. And this is not to
mean a single world-wide
culture of beautiful and
aggregated variations. That
pleasantry was a romantic hope,
not an ideal, but a hope that
never was. This is a syncretic
and synthesized expression of
the Sign and the Value
associated with Signs as
culture-static. This culture
in stasis, to repeat, is
ceaseless and endless in its

homogeneity of revelation as
expressed through individuals,
groups, nations, empires, and
species. So, what are we to
expect? What are we waiting
for?

     We are waiting for the
real. One could say it is all
around us, others will say it
is illusion and what we
perceive only masks the true
real to be unveiled from the
lifting the Maya of the East.

Others in science may lay arms
on the argument to subjective
relativity on a quantum level.
These are all based on a
History that never was and yet
never will end. It is this
dichotomy that may cause a
sense of cognitive dissonance
for the social, for how could
History exist ad-infinitum if
it has no precession?
Simulation Theory brings us
close with its Xerox/Mythos of
a copy with no origin. Close
yes; however, more to the point

is a fable with no origin. A
copy is a representation, yet a
fable represents a story, a
history. This is what we
encounter, a fabled history
with a specific content that is
without origin.

  This theory of a precession of
the simulacra aides us in
understanding the contemporary
milieu of a fabled history
without origin. One could say
there was in fact original
authorship to the Fable of

Washington's chopping of the
Cherry tree and his refusal of
a lie. However, since the story
in fact has no historic
backbone or accuracy, it is in
fact an embedded lie itself
into the modern culture stream
of todays endless network of
half-truths at best and fake/
news propaganda at it's worst.
It is essentially falsehood in
a sea of falsity. Enter the
fairytale. Enter the dragon of
illusion from the desks of
youth to the info/wars of

millennials through to the elders in the demographic expression. Today we are at the precipice of the Unknown Dawn. These are the shadow-lands where truth and fiction blend so seamlessly via a conglomerate of algorithms where aggregate aptitudes of discernment near a Nexus-point of not-knowing so great that soon no-one will have a fighting chance at self-defining truth from falsity. These so called info-wars are

deadly, silent, and hence
dangerous and unknown to the
vast majority. Often absorbed
and digested through malignant
suggestions of disinformation.

The moral and ethical
superstructures of culture have
faded like an old receipt in
the wallet of mankind. The
thermal paper only offering
blurred lines and portions of
the past transaction, with
obliterated content and only
clues to be deciphered as to

the original's testament.
Hence, there is no longer any
check on an ethical treatment
of the science-tech algorithms
and their reflective effect on
the end-user (user as addict).

Take for instance a user with
smart/watch, smart/phone,
smart/tv, smart home/
surveillance system, and smart/
streaming audio receiver; how
smart is this scenario? Aside
from any claims of this
argument having Luddite
origins, be it known, this

scenario is more common than
not, and so intrusive, so
complete, it demands attention
as to whether these smart
services are in fact
worthwhile. The answer is no,
emphatically. And yet if you
turn them off, in today's
atmosphere, it would appear
like a camel with its head in
the sand. Is there a
compromise, a way of using said
services at a point of less
risk? Let us return to this
global-risk question later and

work more precisely and deeply
with one aspect listed above,
that of the smart phone and
social media outlets and
inlets. These are the currents
and tides of the cultural
implosion that lead to the
Singularity.

  Here is the culmination of the
Cyber-culture-war among us;
With each user receiving
tailored content at the
illusion of a stable,
universal, content, the user is

deceived from the first click,
the first like, the first
follow. Like a casino, the
house always wins. In today's
sphere of socialized media, the
user thinks they are
encountering a world wide web,
yet in fact they are caught
within the web of persuasion,
group-think, endless user-
pressure, false representations
of signs, and of course,
targeted advertising.

This phantom of the panopticon, this stressor of images and sounds in constant flux, leads the user to either a sea-sickness, or a euphoria. These two outcomes define the nature of both a stay in Las Vegas, and the lifestyle of the user in the current social media hysteria. Yes, hysteria, for now the slew of smart phones and smart devices has reached a point where the waitress is literally pouring the coffee all over the table, the mug overflowing with the caffeinated excess of stimulation. We are over stimulated, overcome with the tech-spectacle and ready to launch. But launch to where? For if our history never was, then how can there be a when, not to mention a where?

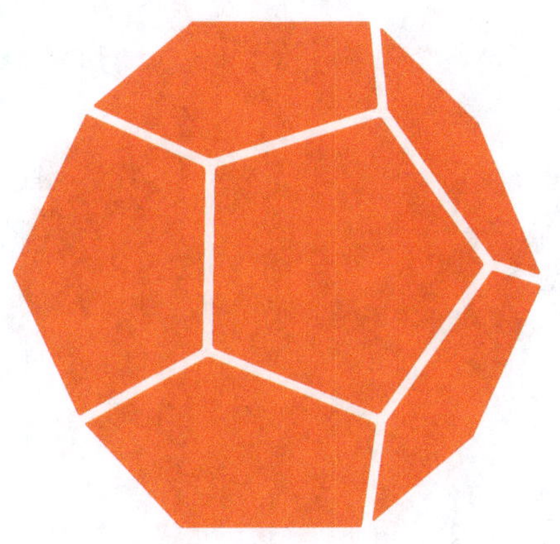

BOOK III. EUPHORIA MORNING

This sense of euphoric awe at the spectacle of culture rolling within itself, and the horror of Oblivion and loss of Cultural Self at the hands of the omniscient grid of tech-hegemony appear polarities and in opposition. Opposed, yet nonetheless, both are integrated fully into the Singularity of the modern global Cultus. This occurs via

the fragmentation of the
culture occurring
simultaneously with it's
conglomeration. Like the
Hermetic axiom, "as above, so
below", the individual mirrors
the culture at large. As the
culture expands into infinite
modalities of being, there is
euphoric ecstasy given the
scale of hyper-transfiguration,
yet likewise, shock and
disillusionment from the loss
of pre-singular culture, ie.
the "neighborhood" or sense of

the local, for example. Hence,
at an individual level, the
psyche is in a latent state of
cognitive dissonance given this
loss of self into the
marketplace of infinite value
transactions where they have
become commodity, and
concurrently are seduced by
this metamorphosis. It is the
seduction of change; change
from a world that was static.
The old guard of empires,
feudal homes, nation/states,
civil-wars, social revolutions,

rebellions, espionage,
Hollywood re-enactments,... all
these static elements implode
into the new era of post-global
controlled chaos. This chaos,
controlled via tethered
networks of information
modules, only becomes more
chaotic as the control
mechanism self-perfects. Here,
the gears and levers of the
machinery are self-perfecting
with algorithms of AI so
quickly, and with such speed,
that both the agony and the

ecstasy of both the individual
and the Mass of humanity are
Co-incident(the euphoria and
the crash occurring
simultaneously and constantly).

This flux of ecstasy and agony
places both the Singularity and
the individual in a state of
elated panic. Overwhelmed and
overstimulated, both enter
fight or flight
psychologically. This is
damaging, for a constant state
of elevated panic and euphoria,

as in the case of fight or
flight, takes an energetic and
emotional expense on the
individual, and at large, in
the greater Cultus, a post-high
come-down like an addict losing
dopamine. The effect is
numbness, an apathy, an atrophy
of reason and activity.
Ironically, at the same time,
the speed of information and
value transactions in the
Singularity also create more
activity and a mania. Thus we
have both man and mankind in a

static state of activity and
inactivity. This is action void
of meaning. Action for the sake
of more action in a never-
ending mobius-strip of
exhausted entertainment. For
this is what activity for no
reason is: leisure. This
leisure, this sense of behavior
modified only through a sense
of entertainment is the true
sense of the "Circus of
Humanity". This circus, with
dazzling heights, side-shows,
refreshments, and jugglers,

does have a paid admission.
All are welcome, in fact all
are present. No one can leave
the Masters Chambers in the
hotel phantasmagoria that hosts
the Carnival of the
Singularity.

   Given this disastrous
psychological trance of apathy,
coupled with a grip of
rebellion, we encounter the
zeitgeist, the current essence
of the (un)real. Here we find
the outsider with too much

inside information. We have the
neophyte with the keys to the
kingdom, and a terminal with no
termed terminus. Is this the
modern condition of the 20th
Century interlocked with the
worldwide global pandemic of
the 21st century? We could only
wish. For that would just be an
extension of the dissolving
social intrigued with it's own
illness. We all are pandemic.
We all are the outsider. We all
have dissolved into the
disinfectant of the virus. Yet

not a biological virus. We're
are suffering from the viral
video, the viral headline, the
computer virus. Yet there is no
anti-virus software to save us.
Mostly since we do not need
saving. We have become free
from the fetters of a History
which subjugated and enslaved,
raped and ravaged, and
ultimately blinded us with a
truth in fiction. No longer
will the diverse and permanent
be dominant. This is the end of
time and the entrance of the

floating freedom of
Singularity, where time and
History, past and present,
Fable and truth in fiction are
obsolete. This obsolescence is
driven steadily like steam from
an engine of hope where ones
freedom is dictated by their
ability to overcome the history
of History. The Singularity, as
event, also is a transaction
with value and hence absorbed
in itself. To see this
possibility, the outsider can
determine their own fate,

determine their own history, their own philosophy, religion, politics, reality. This is not delusion. Neither is this escaping the matrices of Medusa and her media-monster. It is simply forgetting. To forget, create, and become; this is the Euphoria Morning of the Unknown Dawn. The beginning of one's self; The great escape of the Singularity, is to first become the awareness of this loss of a cultural context, and be. Whatever that may be.

BOOK IV.
(EN)TRANCE

This escape, or rather
(en)trance into becoming,
amidst the Singularity,
requires confronting the
Singularity and becoming just
that. Thus, self imploding into
nothingness to recreate oneself
is requisite. This is not

breaking the civil code of the global matrix, or freeing oneself of the permeating hyper-Cultus. It is becoming code, becoming the cybernetic-stasis. Thus, to reach a fulfillment one need the ability to see both sides of the coin at the same time. For this is a unity of opposites. That is to view both the nihilistic depths of nothingness as truth and at the precise moment, see as equal truth it's diametric opposite,

the beautiful emergence of
Global unification at every
value level and transaction in
totality. This beautiful
massacre of a united modality
of thought, the destruction of
isolated thought systems and
contagions, appears to strike
in opposition to the
Singularity, yet
counterintuitively, this split-
screen, dual-viewed reality
gives a more accurate
observance of the nature of

living within the Singularity,
or free from it so to speak.

   Most religious, political,
economic, scientific, or other
traditional variants of culture
demonstrate some aspect or
spectrum of dualistic or
synthetic modalities of
thought. For instance Paganism
vs. Monotheism in the faith
based dynamic of traditional
cultural dynamism. The entrance
into the new, the release from
our post-modern/Singularity,

requires one to view both
perspectives as equally true,
although seemingly in direct
conflict and opposition.
Fortunately, the mind living in
the Singularity is perfectly
primed for this suggestion,
which may, in a sense be
achieved via an auto-suggestion
or Self-hypnotic state. This
would lead to the forgetting.
Followed by creation and
becomingness.

The psyche is primed for this
auto-hypnosis as reflected by
the Mass exposure to infinite
varieties of media-based
sensory blinding encounters
creating the trance state
necessary for admission to the
high estate of release from the
Singularity itself. To catch a
criminal, one must first think
with criminality. To catch a
glimpse at the end of History,
politics, economics, art,
psychology, one must be part
Historian, political scientist,

economist, artist,
psychologist, etc. Then can one
forget the seeming opposition
of Paganism and Monotheism, for
example, and enter the non-
duality needed to unveil the
beautiful melancholy of the
Singularity. Here, one does
kill out desire, and in fact
forget desire, in an effort to
create and enter becomingness.
This is the unraveling of the
Self, that proceeds forth from
an individual and global ego-
death. This is the destiny of

nations, the destiny of personalities. In the fabled entrance to Plato's Academy were inscribed the words, "Know Thyself". These words ring true here as one must know themself in order to lose themselves to the imposing and oppressive omniscience of the current Singularity of Culture. Again, one must perceive, then truly understand and know that they are themselves and yet at the same time not themselves. It is leveraging two opposing ideas

and truths and accepting both
as equally true. For in a world
void of Truth, one must accept
that void as a reality, create
a truth, and become the end-
point of that conclusion.
Morality and immorality would
likewise fall into this process
seeing both the right and the
wrong, the good beyond evil, as
obsolete and at the same time
absolute. As to the emergence
and entrance into becomingness
given the Cultural Singularity,
in sum, the user must become

the menace of the Medusa-Media-
Machine, and, simultaneously,
be the Elegant Aesthetic Good
which is the Cybernetic Unified
Field Cult of the modern era.
This takes a very discerning
and brave psychological
profile. Yet, the Singularity
admits all, and although none
can leave it's grasp, all can
become an emergent threat at
it's very existence. For, as
some fight fire with fire and
forge anew a greater Light, so
culture, at the cusp of a new

Round, can implode and burst
with all looking within.

BOOK V. TRANSMISSION

All are uniquely qualified
to hear the universal call to
action; every person entwined
in the Cultural Singularity
has embedded within them the
ability to view, and hence on
a quantum level of
abstraction, alter the
Singularity and themselves.

This ability at alteration is derived from being a piece of the interconnected supra-structure of the current Social Variant. In Monotheism, being a part of God reveals ones personal divinity, and in nihilism, being a part of nothingness ensures non-being at the individual level at its fullest extension. Within the Cultural Singularity, being a part of that Unity, one finds

their own unique completeness
and totality of singular
personality and
individuation. We are not
discussing anything other
than personal Freedom per se,
for anything other than that
implies Freedom from some
"thing" or structure or
individual. This is a
personal liberation of the
Self from the not-self.
Contemplating freeing oneself
from oneself leans one to

Eastern Traditions and modes
of being. However, this is
not the case of the monk at
the Mountain-top, in
meditation deep, reflecting
on raising consciousness to
Divine atmospheres. This is
finding ones place in the
ultra-violence of the
beautiful and oppressive
matrix of the Cyber-Media-
Cultus, and becoming just
that, in order to view
oneself and ultimately alter

that being through the act of self-viewing. As mentioned earlier, at the Quantum level, a viewpoint directed at any object changes it's nature and hence behavior. Thus, truly viewing oneself within the Cultural Singularity, which is static, would enable one to create alterity, and in a sense, create a new and moving behavior imprint within a seemingly static structure.

It is making the statue move.
It is magico-mystical at an
extremely tech-driven level
of Cultural control.
Mirroring this Social control
mechanism is the self-control
or discipline of the user/
agent/individual. Without
first losing that agency, one
cannot regain and later alter
it in a process of
becomingness or transmutation
into the new. This is the
modern/post-modern alchemy

needed in the remainder of
the 21st Century. The sulphur
and mercury of the
alchemists, and their
resulting spiritual gold,
have now transmuted into
data-servers, media-virality,
and dark-matter; the modern
elixirs of creative self-
generation and rebellion
unfurling.

The magical alchemists
agreed to turn the physical

man into the spiritual. The
current era demands one to
likewise transform; the goal
is to drive from the
Singularity to a transmission
state of integration, in
order to become the "beyond".
Not metaphysical. Beyond.
Implicit in the term beyond
is being past something. This
is the crux of the modern
cultural dilemma: To move
past it. We must cross over
the cultural definitions,

Dynamics, Histories, Traditions, Understandings, in order to move to the beyond. This is the mid-region of neither here nor there. It is void of space and time. This is the argument and goal of the sages and philosophers of fabled eras gone by. To achieve complete command of the elements, the physical, mental, and supra-mental states of being. Of completing the ontological strictures of act and potency. This does involve action, potent action.

How does an individual sacrifice agency to gain capacity? Through going to the root of the agency and through that inner-working, find the source of the Singularity that is omnipresent and yet imploding into nothingness simultaneously. One could

jump to ancient and modern
events and histories to
explain the current
zeitgeist. This would be in
error. We now know the
relativity of time and space.
Hence looking anywhere other
than "now" is fruitless. Now
defends itself. Now knocks at
every door. For the now is
and always was. This brings
one to the "I am that I
am" of lore. "I am that".
Better.... "I am now".

Removing agency, one can find the universal key to understanding their place in the infinite vistas of the supra-saturated, apathy bending, and cyber-spiraling ocean of Singularity. I AM NOW. This is not an agency, capacity, or ability. This is now and I am now. There is a force to this. There is a command. There is an understanding. Yet there is no room for reasonable debate. I am now. No more, no less. Once this is achieved, knowing the truth of "I am now", one must view the other side of the coin. The opposing truth that hurts. The I am not now. The negation of agency, capacity, and ability. This is quite a dizzying truth to complete. Nonetheless, if one attempts, it is possible to truly view ones not-self, that is their non-being. Not insignificance, but non-being. With these two truths embodied, I AM NOW/ I AM NOT, one finds the brutal truth of the binary nature of the most simple code to be broken. It was once said, "HE WHO TRIES TO PENETRATE INTO THE PHILOSOPHICAL ROSE GARDEN WITHOUT A KEY, RESEMBLES A MAN WHO WANTS TO WALK WITHOUT FEET." This is the determination required to crack the simple code:1.0.

This is not the Baconian "To be or not to be?". This is not a a question but an Estate. It is the Kingdom of Being. It is and ever was. Post-history, post-culture, post-Singularity; this is Now.

BOOK VI.
POETRY

IDOLOFTHESPIDERSWEB

Cloaked in darkness fair,

entwined in the doubled lair,

the beast parade hath set him

near,

to terror's destined

atmosphere.

The vacant brow, the muffled

tongue,

none forget the web begun,

the rise and turn of a

tempests tale,

where a ventrilouquist is hid

for sale.

With a spiders grin in

language weak,

the public dole their food
for sheep,
skinned and yoked a tyrants
fool,
the colloseum doth make them
drool.
With shackles and feet
unfettered,
the mainstreet markets shall
be bettered.
But none can rise on legs so
weak,

and lead a ship that harbors

deep.

A honey suckle sickle

smashed,

the spiders groan is heard at

last.

Yet not forget the ancient

tale,

of a soul and sin prepared

for sale,

to daemons bright with

morning stars,

the child of Faust behind
gold bars.
For to put forth this wicked
course,
with votes and bills of one's
remorse.
The builders planned and
checked the set,
of stars unknown and planets
yet,
discovered and wakened long,

the time hath brought this
beast along.

Not in a name or nocturns
pull,

No alchemy can stop the
shrill,

the voices heard the figure
stands,

as one whose spider's hands
demands.

For to errupt with passive
tones,

only sets the stage alone,

for the killing of the

spiders web,

it's idols, caverns, markets

dead.

The cleaving of the freedom

spell,

hath fallen into hands of

hell.

The sorcery of those that

pull,

the spiders whisp is what
will tell.
No recourse for a bend in
time,
no turning pages back in
ryhme,
the spider is before our
court,
what must be done of poisons
sort?
But tamper with ye spiders
fill,

and check and balance every
will,
For none should suffer this
rotten test,
of the spiders will that
mocks at best...
The best intentions of this
land,
that heartache struggle did
demand,
with hope of an ancient
promise progress,

to slay the spider involoves

address,

so harken all ye disputed

souls,

and kindly unravel the

tethered polls,

which awaken feelings from

the roots,

that none should conquer with

lack of proof.

A king, a queen, a jester

too,

the forest fills with a clown
of zoos.
Where every day a star in
born,
Lest not forget that some are
worn,
in cloaks unseen and in
shadows scarce,
the face of hell intrudes the
space.
For who could trump the card
at hand,

when every soul's spirit must
demand....
A script, a type, a
puppeteer,
the name is bold, the people
fear,
a tyrant and attacks unknown,
the idol of the spiders web
is shown.
So cast your fetters to the
moon,

and seek for justice high <u>at</u>
<u>noon</u>.
For not to act is action too,
return the spider and the
fool.

RITES OF THE HARVEST

All gather the reaping,

all eyes are seeing,

all turn for the believing,

the harvest brings the dawn,

With tales of sleeping,

with dreams of reaching,

with ears for hearing,

the priestly caste is born.

As Arjuna stands before them,
as the bodhi weeps in stem,
as doves released once
penned,
the yoke of reason leaves.
Then essenian prophets fill,
then mosaic hands reveal,
then revel rivals steal,
the Sun becomes the Son.
With a world enraveled
suffering,

with a word enraged in
smothering,
with unheard of time
unraveling,
the prince becomes the
throne.
A mystic twist of chemistry,
a gypsy's course of majesty,
a concord in the calvary,
the temple's sol invited.
In Plato's den forgotten,
in Athena's hand begotten,

in remembrance of the
trodden,
the flood revives in time.
Invited for the feast,
invited seek the beast,
invited spirits least,
the witches burn in brew.
When legend strikes Molay,
when a table round is stayed,
when specular crowns obey,
the secrets slip from mouth
to ear.

Bring east to west,

bring north at best,

bring south in rest,

the baboon is stuffed for

peering.

If ladders lead to hallowed

heights,

if visions speak in tongues

of ice,

if fire warms the heart in

night,

the harvest brings the dawn.

The harvest brings the dawn,
when seeking searches on,
while paths so true beguile
the mind,
the harvest brings the dawn.
Earned maji majestic of the
greatest heights,
so lonley lead their work in
sight,
if plainly gifts are honored
few,
the harvest brings the dawn.

With lilies trodden
underfoot,
the greatest Copt a secret
put,
in letters L, P, and D,
the harvest brings the dawn.
For what becomes a harvest,
lacking in the dawn,
a rosy cross forgotten?
Or roses on the lawn...
Ask a travelling man from
west to east,

a brother or a self to be,
the harvest lies in all of
us,
which way we spring the font
of rust.
The Harvest Brings The Dawn

ON CASUISTRY

Fickle finds remove labors
lust,

so once removed the actions
trust,

for work in deed for
providence sake,

the leaves of breathing for

the world remain.

The courts of reason do

provide,

a skythe the stone and moral

right,

yet if one pebble overturn,

the case of cases forever

burn.

A sealed casket with earthen

gold,

the law of deadhand a burden
bold,
with assumptions answer the
cracken mind,
yet a rule of one for all
mankind.
Each to his her only stake,
a truth so known its meaning
made,
a grecian urn a world will
fade,

the lamplit sky a subjects
fate.
To catch a pike in many
halls,
Versaille is crying neath her
walls,
a mirror of a shadows lense,
to ask oneself what may
depend.
For if a soul can trust
itself,

need reason or a reference
shelf,
the battered thoughts of
purile bones,
the thoughts that make one's
mind it's home.
So ask if why and whence and
wither,
A man can shoulder questions
hither,
of where and when was brought
about,

the orb of light a word a
shout.
A syllogistic pulse is
brooding,
to scrape the marrow from the
shooting,
of stars off course and
answers lost,
to know thyself or faith at
cost.
Enliven yearnings but follow
true,

the compass' needle points
for few,

for dark and light are of the
same,

break casuistry and the fools
parade.

As if one knows, no need
believe,

no deal of faith will less
decieve,

A pear falls and strikes the
ground,

I hear it strike, I hear the
sound.

About the Author

Andrew K. Coyne lives in
Altadena, CA, with his wife
Tara and their children Bradley
and Kali. Andrew studied
Politics and Philosophy at the
University of California at Los
Angeles and has a deep rooted
passion for ancient and modern
metaphysics.